Light a Candle for All to

Unison or Two-part any Combination
with opt. Congregation and Narration*
for each Advent Sunday and Christmas Eve or Chris

by **Lloyd Larson**

*Performance options, information for the Congregation part (p. 13-14) and the Narrations (p. 15-16)
are included as indicated.

10/4655L

Unison or Two-part any Combination with opt. Congregation and Narration

Light a Candle for All to See

Words and Music by

Lloyd Larson

Usage:
Advent/Christmas

Scripture references:
Psalm 146:5-10; Isaiah 9:2-7; Micah 5:4-5; Luke 2:8-20;
John 1:1-5

Lorenz Company • www.lorenz.com

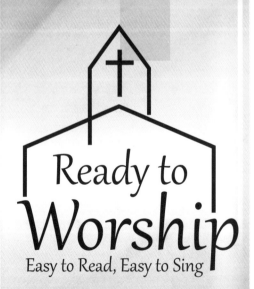

Ready to
Worship
Easy to Read, Easy to Sing

kings and Lord of lords! Come

fill our hearts with Your hope and
peace
love
joy
light

reign for - ev - er - more.

6

Hope Narration: "I know the plans I have for you," declares the Lord, "plans to prosper you

38

and not to harm you, plans to give you hope and a future." *(Jeremiah 29:11)*

41

Put your hope in the Lord, for with the Lord is unfailing

44

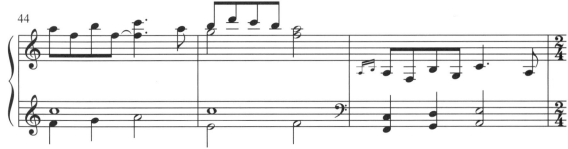

love, and with Him is full redemption *(Psalm 130:7)*

47

Blessed is the one whose help is in the God of Jacob, whose hope is in the Lord,

50

*The narration for each service (Hope, Peace, Love, Joy and Light) is read while the music is played in measures 38-55. If narration is not used, the interlude may begin at M 50 using the second ending.

the Maker of heaven and earth—the Lord, Who remains faithful forever. *(Psalm 146:5-6)*

* You may repeat to measure 38 or 50 as needed.

8

10/4655L-8

man - u - el.
man - u - el.
man - u - el.
man - u - el.
man - u - el.

And

End - less hope: Em - man - u - el.
Prince of peace: Em - man - u - el.
Gift of love: Em - man - u - el.
Bound - less joy: Em - man - u - el.
Light of life: Em - man - u - el.

with us He___ shall ev - er dwell.

And

10

with us He shall ev - er dwell. Em

man - u - el: God with

man - u - el: God with

us, King of kings and Lord of

us, King of kings and Lord of

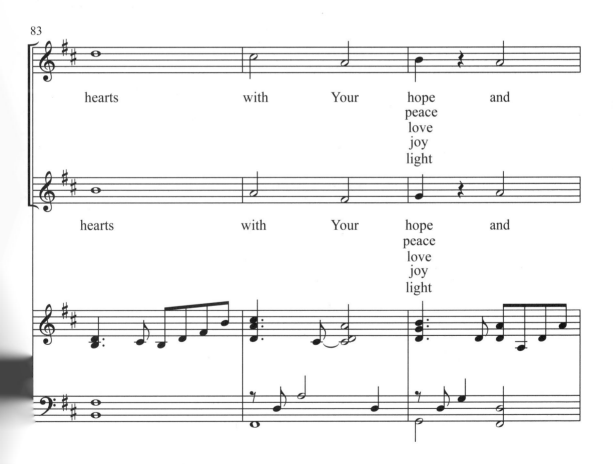

12

Light a Candle for All to See

Congregation – *Hope*
Words and Music by Lloyd Larson

Please sing when directed
(Sing the echo)
Light a candle for all to see. *(Light a candle for all to see.)*
The King shall come for you and me. *(The King shall come for you and me.)*
Endless hope: Emmanuel. *(Endless hope: Emmanuel.)*
And with us He shall ever dwell. *(And with us He shall ever dwell.)*

(All sing)
Emmanuel: God with us, King of kings and Lord of lords!
Come fill our hearts with Your hope and reign forevermore.

Light a Candle for All to See

Congregation – *Peace*
Words and Music by Lloyd Larson

Please sing when directed
(Sing the echo)
Light a candle for all to see. *(Light a candle for all to see.)*
The King shall come for you and me. *(The King shall come for you and me.)*
Prince of peace: Emmanuel. *(Prince of peace: Emmanuel.)*
And with us He shall ever dwell. *(And with us He shall ever dwell.)*

(All sing)
Emmanuel: God with us, King of kings and Lord of lords!
Come fill our hearts with Your peace and reign forevermore.

Light a Candle for All to See

Congregation – *Love*
Words and Music by Lloyd Larson

Please sing when directed
(Sing the echo)
Light a candle for all to see. *(Light a candle for all to see.)*
The King shall come for you and me. *(The King shall come for you and me.)*
Gift of love: Emmanuel. *(Gift of love: Emmanuel.)*
And with us He shall ever dwell. *(And with us He shall ever dwell.)*

(All sing)
Emmanuel: God with us, King of kings and Lord of lords!
Come fill our hearts with Your love and reign forevermore.

Light a Candle for All to See

Congregation – *Joy*
Words and Music by Lloyd Larson

Please sing when directed
(Sing the echo)
Light a candle for all to see. *(Light a candle for all to see.)*
The King shall come for you and me. *(The King shall come for you and me.)*
Boundless joy: Emmanuel. *(Boundless joy: Emmanuel.)*
And with us He shall ever dwell. *(And with us He shall ever dwell.)*

(All sing)
Emmanuel: God with us, King of kings and Lord of lords!
Come fill our hearts with Your joy and reign forevermore.

Light a Candle for All to See

Congregation – *Light*
Words and Music by Lloyd Larson

Please sing when directed
(Sing the echo)
Light a candle for all to see. *(Light a candle for all to see.)*
The King shall come for you and me. *(The King shall come for you and me.)*
Light of life: Emmanuel. *(Light of life: Emmanuel.)*
And with us He shall ever dwell. *(And with us He shall ever dwell.)*

(All sing)
Emmanuel: God with us, King of kings and Lord of lords!
Come fill our hearts with Your light and reign forevermore.

Light a Candle for All to See

Narration for each Advent Sunday and Christmas Eve or Christmas Day

The following narrations may be read by one or more readers during the interlude for *Light a Candle for All to See* (measures 38–55). They may be lengthened or abbreviated as desired. Feel free to employ other scriptures or readings as appropriate to individual worship needs. The scripture references should not be read as part of the narration.

Hope (Advent #1)

"I know the plans I have for you," declares the Lord, "plans to prosper you and not to harm you, plans to give you hope and a future." *(Jeremiah 29:11)*

Put your hope in the Lord, for with the Lord is unfailing love and with Him is full redemption. *(Psalm 130:7)*

Blessed is the one whose help is the God of Jacob, whose hope is in the Lord, the Maker of heaven and earth—the Lord, who remains faithful forever. *(Psalm 146:5-6)*

Peace (Advent #2)

For unto us a Child is born, unto us a Son is given; and the government shall be upon His shoulder, and His name shall be called "Wonderful Counselor, Mighty God, Everlasting Father, the Prince of Peace." *(Isaiah 9:6)*

He shall stand and feed His flock in the strength of the Lord, in the majesty of the name of the Lord His God. And His people shall dwell secure, for He shall be great to the ends of the earth. And He will be their peace. *(Micah 5:4-5)*

Love (Advent #3)

I will sing of the Lord's great love forever; with my mouth I will proclaim Your faithfulness to all generations. I will declare that Your steadfast love stands firm forever, that Your faithfulness is as firm as the heavens. *(Psalm 89:1-2)*

The Lord appeared to us in the past, saying: "I have loved you with an everlasting love; I have drawn you with loving-kindness." *(Jeremiah 31:3)*

"God so loved the world that He gave His only Son, so that everyone who believes in Him may not perish but may have eternal life." *(John 3:16)*

Joy (Advent #4)

Shout for joy to the Lord, all the earth. Worship the Lord with gladness; come before Him with joyful songs. *(Psalm 100:1-2)*

In that region there were shepherds living in the fields, keeping watch over their flock by night. Then an angel of the Lord stood before them, and the glory of the Lord shone around them, and they were terrified. But the angel said to them, "Do not be afraid. I bring you good news of great joy for all the people. Today in the town of David a Savior has been born to you. He is Christ the Lord." *(Luke 2:8-11)*

Light (Christmas Eve or Christmas Day)

The people walking in darkness have seen a great light; on those living in the land of the shadow of death a light has dawned. *(Isaiah 9:2)*

The sun will no more be your light by day, nor will the brightness of the moon shine on you, for the Lord will be your everlasting light, and your God will be your glory. *(Isaiah 60:19)*

In the beginning was the Word, and the Word was with God, and the Word was God. He was with God in the beginning. In Him was life, and that life was the light to all people. The light shines in the darkness, but the darkness has not understood it. *(John 1:1-2, 4-5)*

10/4655L-16